I0160067

# Practical Guide to the Operational Use of the Remington 870 Shotgun

By Erik Lawrence

Copyright ©2014 Erik Lawrence

ATTENTION US MILITARY UNITS, US GOVERNMENT AGENCIES AND PROFESSIONAL ORGANIZATIONS: Quantity discounts are available on bulk purchases of this book. Special books or book excerpts can also be created to fit specific needs. For information, please contact:

Erik Lawrence
www.vig-sec.com     erik@vig-sec.com

Although the author and publisher have made every effort to ensure the accuracy and completeness of information contained in this book, we assume no responsibility for the use or misuse of information contained in this book, errors, inaccuracies, omissions, or any inconsistency herein. Portions of this manual are excerpts from outside sources but have been validated and modified as necessary.

**Printed and bound in the United States of America**

**First printing 2012**
**Second printing 2014**

**ISBN 10: 1-941998-14-3**
**ISBN 13: 978-1-941998-14-4**
**EBOOK – ISBN-13:  978-1-941998-33-5**
**LCCN: Not yet assigned**

Firearms are potentially dangerous and must be handled responsibly by individuals. The technical information presented in this publication on the use of this weapon reflects the author's research, beliefs, and experiences. The information in this book is presented for academic study only. Neither the author nor the publisher assumes any responsibility for the use or misuse of information contained in this book.

**SAFETY NOTICE -** Before starting an inspection, ensure the weapon is cleared. Do not manipulate the trigger until the weapon has been cleared of all ammunition. Inspect the chamber to ensure that it is empty and no ammunition is present. Keep the weapon oriented in a safe direction when loading and handling.

**AMMUNITION NOTICE** - This weapon fires the 12-Gauge 2¾-and 3-inch shotshells. Firing the incorrect ammunition will damage the weapon and possibly injure the operator.

**PROPER TRAINING** - Training should be received from knowledgeable and experienced operators on this particular weapons system. Vigilant Security Services, LLC Training provides this training and continually perfects its instruction with up-to-date information from actual use.

**www.vig-sec.com**

# PREFACE

This manual is intended to be a reference for those involved in the use, maintenance and instruction of the featured firearm. My aim in writing these manuals is to set the record straight and dispel many of the false assumptions related to the different firearms. The early sections of the manual contain background material on the featured firearm which allows the user to gain the basic building blocks for further education. The firearms featured in these manuals have been used for decades by our allies and enemies, and will be for the foreseeable future, so why are we not experts with them? If I am fighting with the firearm or providing instruction on a firearm, I want to use and know their system better than they do.

The rationale for writing these manuals comes from the fact that there are not libraries of easily accessible references to use in developing your own training system for these firearms. Many of the old military field manuals are decades old and were incorrectly translated by someone who had no idea what the firearm could do, let alone basic firearm knowledge. We started from the ground up and developed the manuals to provide instruction in progressive steps that could be easily grasped and continually referred back to. A good grounding in the basics of firearms, safety, and instruction allows the user to use these manuals to their maximum value. A competent user will find little difficulty in interpreting and applying the information in the manual to their own training program.

The guide goes through the most fundamental parts of the firearm in detail and more advanced techniques are not covered as extensively. With this in mind the user can use these principles and adapt it as needed to their required level of instruction. The emphasis of this guide is in acquiring familiarity with the fundamentals of all firearms and learned competence rather than becoming a firearms guru.

Many of the points in these guides were developed from scratch in theatres of conflict and are continually improved and updated for each edition. I have continually used vetted points from users and professionals in the guides to continually update them to the best known practices for each particular firearm. If it is valid and relevant we will include it in the next edition.

Please note that this guide assumes some familiarity with the basic concepts in firearm safety, gun handling skills, common sense and an ability to process new information. Readers should have knowledge of the difference in calibers, countries of origin, and the knowledge of the priority of the skills needed for development.

I hope you find this work useful and remember that a manual does not replace proper training and hands on experience. Please email comments to erik@vig-sec.com, particularly if you find any errors or glaring omissions.

Erik Lawrence

# Table of Contents

# Remington
# 870

## SHOTGUN

# Section 1

## Introduction

The objective of this manual is to allow the reader to be able to use the Remington pump action shotgun competently. The manual will give the reader background/specifications of the weapon, instructions on its operation, disassembly, and assembly; proper firing procedure; and malfunction/misfire procedures. Operator-level maintenance will also be detailed to allow the reader to understand and become competent in the use and maintenance of the Remington Shotgun.

## Description

The Remington Model 870 is manufactured in the United States by Remington Arms. This weapon is a pump-action shotgun which uses a wide variety of ammunition for a multitude of purposes. It is widely used by law enforcement and military as a defensive weapon and by civilians for target shooting, hunting, and self-defense. The Remington 870 features a bottom-loading, side-ejecting receiver, tubular magazine under the barrel, dual-action bars, internal hammer, and a bolt which locks into an extension in the barrel.

The characteristics of the Remington 870 shotgun

    A. Country of Origin: United States
    B. Military Designation: M870 or 870 Mark 1, 2, 3, 4, 5, or 6 depending on features.
    C. Cartridge Type: 12-Gauge shotshell, 2¾" and 3" lengths and also for civilian models- 16, 28, 20, and .410 gauge
    D. Weight: 6.6-7.7 pounds/3-3.5 kg
    E. Length
        a. Overall: Varies
        b. Barrel: 10" to 26", depending on requirements
    F. Type of Feed: Tubular magazine
        a. Magazine capacity: 3-8 shells, depending on model and shell length
    G. System of Operation: Pump-action
    H. Maximum Effective Range:
        a. Shotshell 00 Buck- 45 meters
        b. Shotshell Slug- 100 meters
        c. Shotshell #7 shot- 40 meters

## Background

The Remington 870 model was the fourth major design in a series of Remington pump shotguns. John Pedersen designed the Model 10 (and later the improved model 29). Working with John Browning, Pedersen also helped design the Model 17, which was adopted by Ithaca as the Ithaca 37 and also served as the basis for the Remington 31. Remington sought to correct that by introducing in 1950 a modern, streamlined, rugged, reliable, and relatively inexpensive shotgun, the 870 "Wingmaster".

The Remington 870 Wingmaster was introduced by Remington in 1950 and since then has become one of the most popular USA-made pump-action all-purpose shotguns. The 870 began its life as a versatile hunting shotgun available in many different configurations and gauges. Adopted in 1966 by the US Marine Corps and in the early 1970s it was adopted by the US Army. They purchased thousands of the Remington 870 Mk1 shoguns. Military shotguns usually have extended magazines for 7 or 8 rounds; bayonet mounts; heat shields around the barrels; and non-glare, protective, and rust-resistant finishes.

The Remington 870 is also a very popular police/security shotgun, available with extended magazines (up to 8 rounds), fixed or folding buttstocks or pistol grips. Usually, police Remington shotguns have 14-inch or 18-inch barrels with cylinder or improved cylinder chokes, capable of firing buckshot, slugs, and special-purpose munitions (tear gas grenades, non-lethal rubber bullets, etc.). 870s may be equipped with rifle-style or ghost-ring (peep) sights with tactical flashlights and lasers.

## Design

The Remington 870 is a manually operated, pump-action shotgun with dual-action bars and a tilting breech lock, which locks directly into the barrel extension. The barrel may be changed within minutes to fit the shooting situation/shell selection. The tubular magazine is located under the barrel, and depending on the version and gauge, may hold from 3 to 8 cartridges. Sights also are different depending on the purpose and version of the gun, which could include front bead only, rifle-type sights with open notch, ghost ring rear sight, and mounts for various red-dot and other optical sights.

## Operation

The weapon has a single barrel above the magazine tube which holds between 3 and 8 shells, depending on the model. New shells are loaded by pulling a pump handle attached to the cartridge tube toward the operator, then pushing it back into place to insert the cartridge into the chamber. This action simultaneously ejects the most recently fired casing out the side ejection port.

## Variants

There are numerous variations of the Remington 870 shotgun. From the original 15 models offered, Remington currently produces dozens of models for civilian, law enforcement, and military sales. Remington 870 variants can be grouped into

- *Wingmaster* shotguns, featuring polished bluing and glossy wood finishes.
- *Express* models, featuring a bead-blasted finish and satin wood or synthetic furniture.
- *Marine* guns, which have synthetic stocks and nickel finish.
- *Tactical/Police/Military* shotguns, featuring blued or parkerized finishes and satin wood or synthetic stocks.

## Remington 870 Wingmaster

**Figure 1-1 Remington 870 Wingmaster**

**Caliber:** 12-, 28-, 20-, and .410 bore

**Type:** Pump-action

Overall length, weight, barrel length, and magazine capacity are dependent upon a variety of options.

## Remington 870 Express

**Figure 1-2 Remington 870 Express**

**Figure 1-3 Remington 870 Express Combo**

**Caliber:** 12-, 28-, 20-, and .410 bore

**Type:** Pump-action

Overall length, weight, barrel length, and magazine capacity are dependent upon a variety of options.

Offered with a wide selection of gauges and barrel configurations, all wood and metal surfaces have a non-reflective, non-revealing finish. The 12- and 20-gauge models are offered with your choice of a 26- or 28-inch barrel with a Modified Rem Choke. The 28-gauge and .410-bore versions feature 25-inch barrels with a fixed choke.

## Remington 870 Marine Magnum

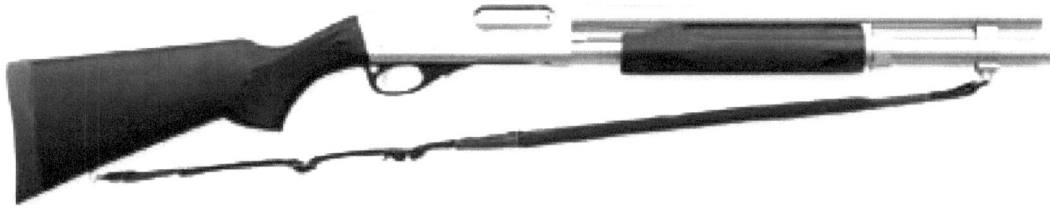

**Figure 1-4 Remington 870 Marine Magnum**

**Caliber:** 12 gauge

**Type:** Pump-action

**Overall length:** 38.5 in/ 97 cm

**Barrel length:** 18 in/ 45 cm

**Magazine capacity:** 6 in magazine and one in chamber

A highly durable 12-gauge utility gun that resists corrosion on land or water. Electroless nickel plating covers all metal, including the inside of the barrel and receiver. The synthetic stock has generous checkering for positive control. This 870 comes with an 18" cylinder barrel with single-bead front sight, six-round magazine, swivel studs, and the revolutionary recoil-reducing R3 recoil pad.

## Remington 870 Tactical/LE Model

**Figure 1-5 Remington 870 Tactical, right side**

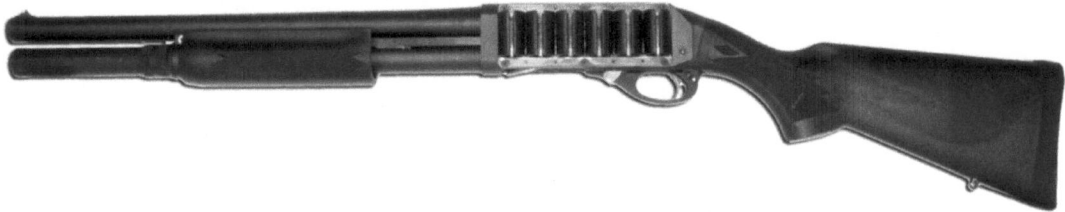

**Figure 1-6 Remington 870 Tactical, left side**

**Caliber:** 12 and 20 gauge

**Type:** Pump-action

**Overall length:** 38 in/ 96 cm

**Barrel length:** 18 in/ 45 cm

**Magazine capacity:** 6 in magazine and one in chamber

The synthetic stock has generous checkering for positive control. This 870 comes with an 18" cylinder barrel with single-bead front sight, six-round magazine, swivel studs, and the revolutionary recoil-reducing R3 recoil pad. Lights and extra shell carriers may be added to kit this shotgun fully to be the best defense shotgun available.

## Remington 870 Modular Combat Shotgun (MCS)

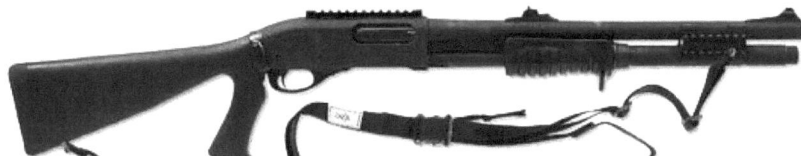

**Figure 1-7 Remington 870 MCS Full-size configuration**

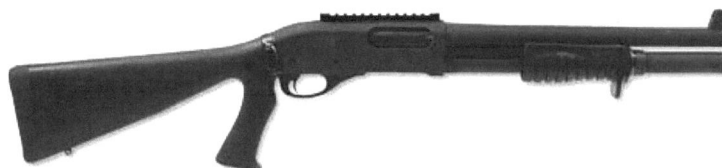

**Figure 1-8 Remington 870 MCS Compact-size configuration**

**Figure 1-9 Remington 870 MCS Breaching tool configuration**

**Figure 1-10 Remington 870 MCS Masterkey configuration**

**Caliber:** 12 gauge

**Type:** Pump-action

**Overall length:** 20" up to 38", depending on the configuration

**Weight unloaded:** 5.6 pounds up to 8 pounds, depending on the configuration.

**Barrel options:** 10" Breacher Tool, 14" Entry/CQB Gun, 18" Patrol Gun, and 10" M4/M16 Accessory Tool

**Magazine capacity:** 5-7 rounds

The latest addition to the M870 line is the 870 Modular Combat Shotgun (MCS). The 870 MCS kit consists of the receiver and magazine tube (3 rounds base capacity), plus several detachable components, such as barrels (10", 14", and 18"), buttstocks (single pistol grip, polymer shoulder stock with pistol grip, polymer shoulder stock with semi-pistol grip), magazine extensions (for total capacity for up to 5 or 7 rounds), and some other accessories. Receiver is fitted with Picatinny rail on top, which can accept various sighting devices, as well as serve as a mount when 870 MCS is used as a modular weapon attached to the M4 carbine or M16 rifle (system generally known as a "Master key" rifle/shotgun combo). In various configurations, the 870 MCS weighs from 5.6 lbs (2.5 kg) in the "M4/M16 accessory shotgun" version with 10" barrel and no buttstock, up to 7.9 lbs (3.6 kg) in the patrol shotgun version with tactical buttstock and 18" barrel.

## Remington 870 Breaching Tool

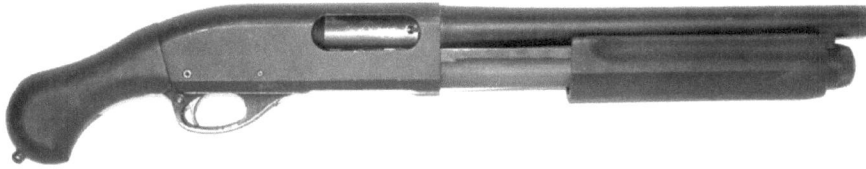

**Figure 1-11 Remington 870 Breaching Tool**

**Caliber:** 12 Gauge

**Type:** Pump Action

**Overall length:** 24 in/ 61 cm

**Weight unloaded:** 5.6 lb/ 2.5 kg

**Barrel length:** 12 in/ 30 cm

**Magazine capacity:** 4 in magazine and one in chamber

The shotgun in this configuration is used by tactical door breachers to separate the hinges and lock mechanisms from the door and the door frame. Use of this firearm/tool must be taught from experienced and qualified instructors as misuse can cause injury to the operator, teammates, and bystanders.

# Section 2

## Maintenance

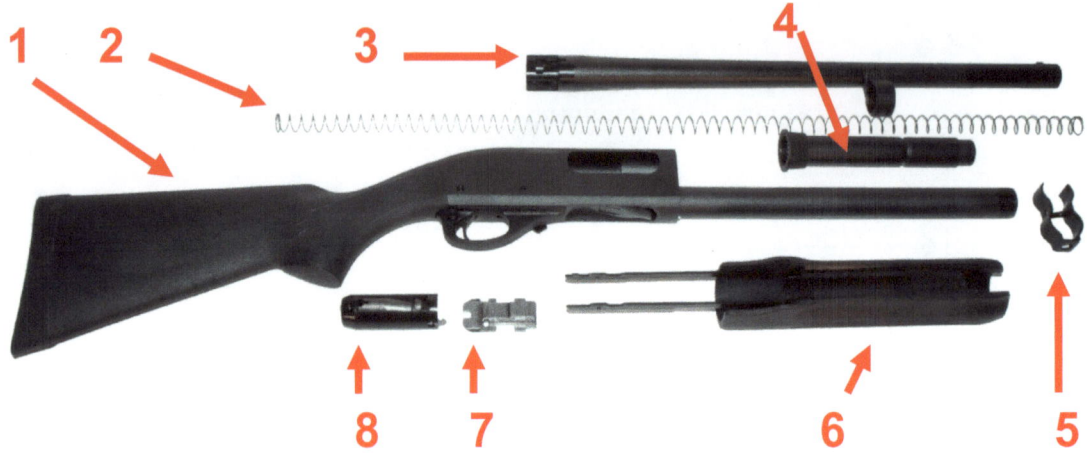

**Figure 2-1 Basic components of a disassembled Remington 870**

1- Stock/Receiver/Magazine Tube Assembly
2- Magazine Spring
3- Barrel
4- Magazine Tube Extension

5- Barrel Band
6- Slide Assembly
7- Slide
8- Breech Bolt

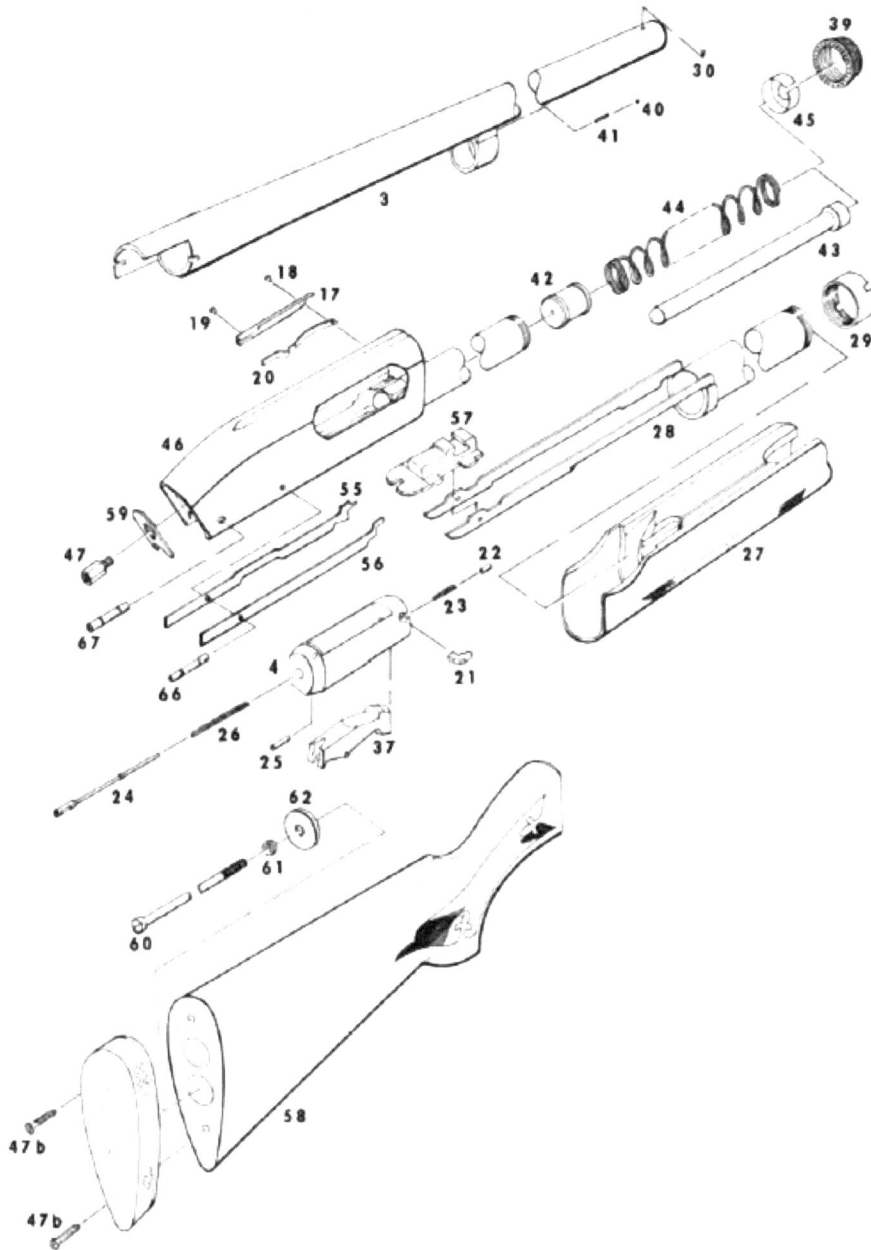

**Figure 2-2 Exploded diagram of the Remington 870 shotgun**

3- Barrel Assembly
4- Breech Bolt/Bolt Assy.
17- Ejector
18- Ejector Rivet, Front
19- Ejector Rivet, Rear
20- Ejector Spring
21- Extractor
22- Extractor Plunger
23- Extractor Spring
24- Firing Pin
25- Firing Pin Retaining Pin
26- Firing Pin Retractor Spring
27- Forend

28- Forend Tube Assembly
29- Forend Tube Nut
30- Front Sight
37- Locking Block Assembly
39- Magazine Cap
40- Magazine Cap Detent
41- Magazine Cap Detent Spring
42- Magazine Follower
43- Magazine Plug – 3 shot
44- Magazine Spring
45- Magazine Spring Retainer
46- Receiver Assembly
47- Receiver Stud

47b- Recoil Pad Screws
55- Shell Latch, Left
56- Shell Latch, Right
57- Slide
58- Stock Assembly
59- Stock Bearing Plate
60- Stock Bolt
61- Stock Lock Washer
62- Stock Bolt Washer
66- Trigger Plate Pin, Front
67- Trigger Plate Pin, Rear

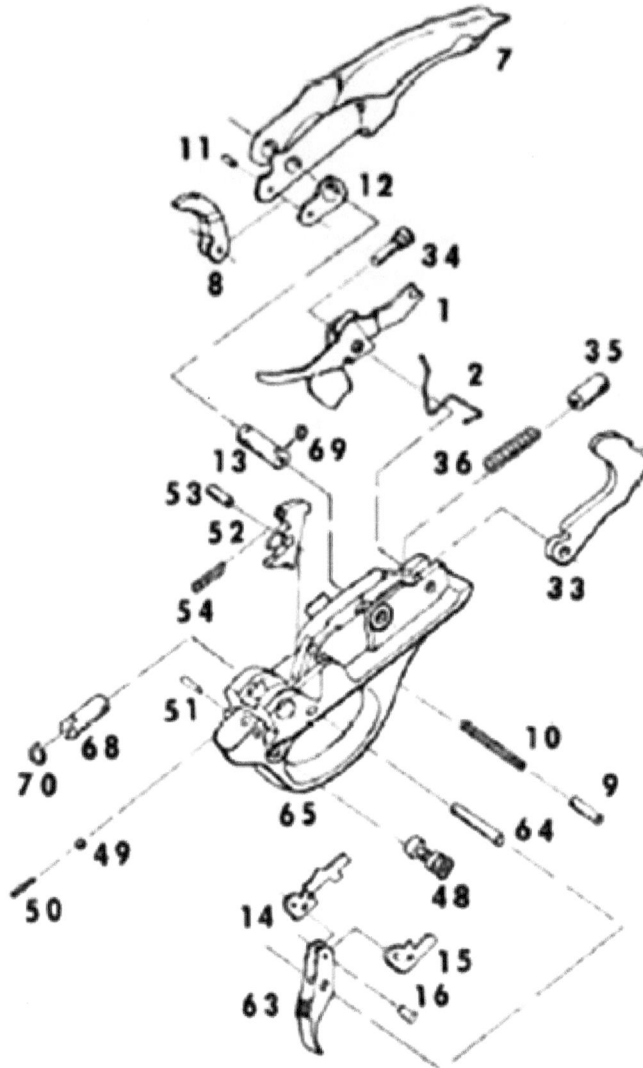

**Figure 2-3 Exploded diagram of the Remington 870 shotgun trigger group**

1- Action Bar Lock
2- Action Bar Lock Spring
7- Carrier
8- Carrier Dog
9- Carrier Dog Follower
10- Carrier Dog Follower Spring
11- Carrier Dog Pin
12- Carrier Dog Washer
13- Carrier Pivot Tube
14- Connector, Left
15- Connector, Right

16- Connector Pin
33- Hammer
34- Hammer Pin
35- Hammer Plunger
36- Hammer Spring
48- Safety Mechanism
49- Safety Mechanism Detent Ball
50- Safety Mechanism Spring
51- Safety Mechanism Retaining Pin
52- Sear
53- Sear Pin

54- Sear Spring
63- Trigger Assembly
64- Trigger Pin
65- Trigger Plate Assembly
68- Trigger Plate Pin Bushing
69- T. Plate Pin Detent, Front
70- T. Plate Pin Detent, Rear

## The Security System

The newer Remington firearms are equipped with an integrated security system. The security system enables the owner to lock the safety mechanism on the firearm in the **"SAFE"** position with the use of a special key.

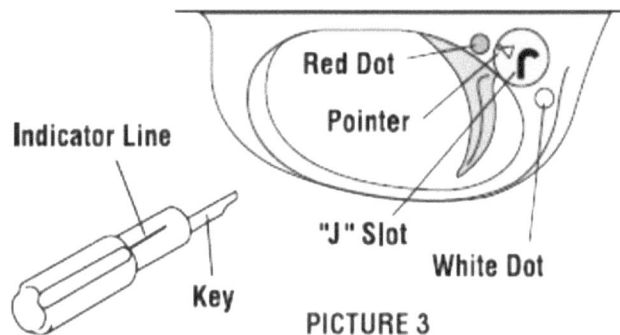

PICTURE 3

**Figure 2-4 Remington Safety System**

The safety mechanism provides additional protection against accidental or unintentional discharge under normal usage when properly engaged and in good working order.

Located on the safety mechanism is a **"J"** shaped slot. This **"J"** slot is the key hole for securing your safety mechanism. Also on the safety mechanism is a pointer which will point and line up with either the **RED** or **WHITE DOT** on the trigger plate when the safety mechanism is turned. The position of the pointer indicates whether or not the security system is engaged. The existence of the security system does not change the basic operation of the safety mechanism, nor does it change the manner in which the safety mechanism should be used (Figure 2-4).

With your new firearm, you will receive a capped key. To use the key, remove the cap. On the key is an indicator line which will line up with the pointer on the safety mechanism.

To engage the security system, press the safety mechanism to the **"SAFE"** position so the **RED BAND DOES NOT SHOW.** Insert the key into the **"J"** slot as far as it can go. Next, turn the key counter-clockwise so that the indicator line on the key and the pointer on the safety mechanism line up with the **WHITE DOT** on the trigger plate. **THE SECURITY SYSTEM IS NOW ENGAGED.**

In operating the security system, **NEVER** use excessive force to turn the key. If the key will not turn freely, contact a Remington authorized repair center.

Keep your security system engaged and your safety mechanism in the **"SAFE"** position when your firearm is not in use. Keep your key in a secure place, inaccessible to others. **DO NOT** leave your key or any ammunition with your firearm, which should be kept unloaded and locked in a safe place.

If you lose the key, **DO NOT** attempt to disengage the safety mechanism using a foreign object. This will damage your firearm. Contact your Remington-authorized dealer for a replacement key.

### Clearing the Remington

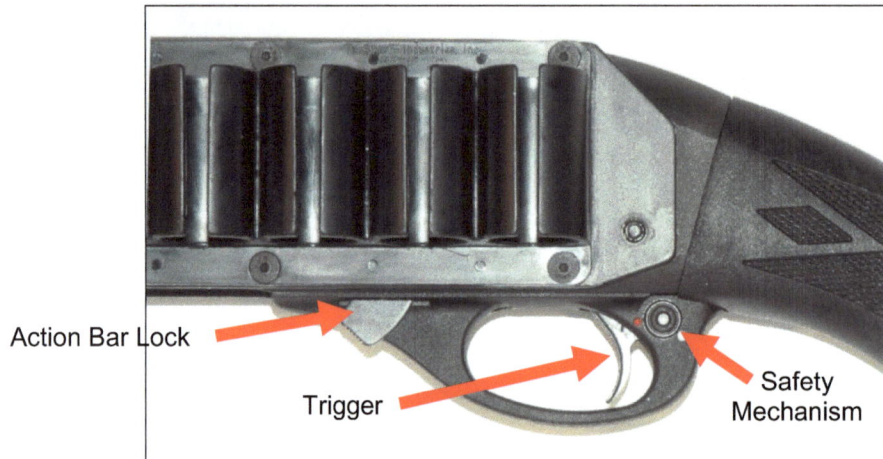

**Figure 2-5 Remington 870 safety, left side**

A. Ensure the shotgun is pointed in a safe direction and the safety is in the **"SAFE"** position. The safety mechanism on the 870 pump-action shotgun is a button located behind the trigger, commonly known as a cross-bolt safety. To engage the safety mechanism, push the button so the **RED BAND MARKING CANNOT BE SEEN, button pressed to the right.**

**Figure 2-6 Cleared magazine tube showing orange follower**

B. Depress the action bar lock and pull the forearm to the rear. Observe any cartridge that is being extracted and ejected from the ejection port. Look into the chamber and magazine tube to see if there are more shotshells present. If more shotshells are in the magazine tube, continue to depress the action bar lock and cycle the action until all shotshells are ejected. Once no more cartridges are being ejected, again observe the chamber and magazine tube. Many of the newer Remington 870s have an orange follower that allows the operator to see that the magazine tube is clear (Figure 2-6).

    a.  Do not attempt to retain the ejected cartridges, pick them up once the shotgun is clear.

    b.  Clean the cartridges prior to loading them at a later time.

**Figure 2-7 Clear chamber and magazine**

C.  Visually and physically check the chamber and magazine tube for rounds (Figure 2-7). Once you have ensured the shotgun has no cartridges in it, you now can close the slide by pushing the forearm forward to the locked position.

## Disassembling the Remington Shotgun

NOTE- Place the shotgun's parts on a flat, clean surface with the muzzle oriented in a safe direction.

When the operator begins to disassemble the shotgun, it should be done in the following order:

A.  Clear the shotgun and leave the safety on; **RED BAND WILL NOT SHOW**.

B.  To remove the magazine cap/magazine tube extension,

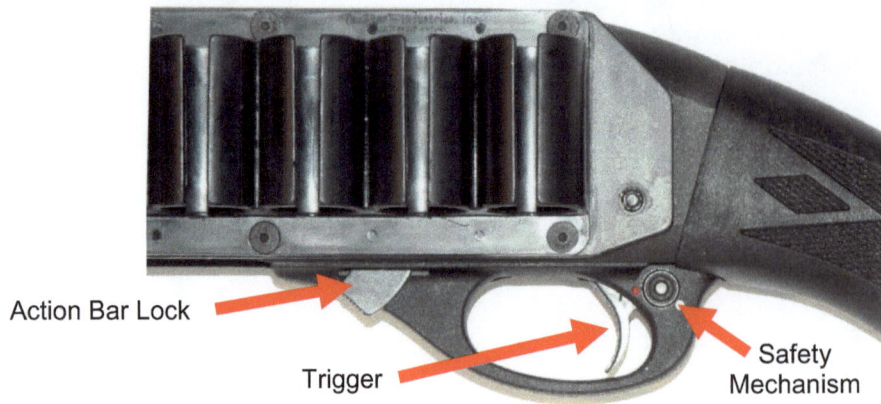

Action Bar Lock

Trigger

Safety
Mechanism

**Figure 2-8**

1. Push the action bar lock upward and pull the fore-end rearward to open the action (Figure 2-8).

2. Slide the fore-end forward approximately halfway.

**Figure 2-9a**

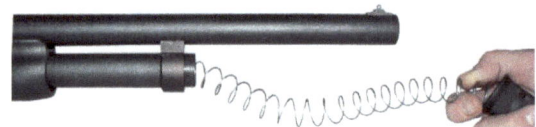

**Figure 2-9b**

3. Unscrew and remove the magazine cap/magazine tube extension (Figure 2-9a). The magazine spring is compressed against the magazine cap/magazine tube extension (Figure 2-9b).

**NOTE:** There are two types of magazine spring retainers when the shotgun does not have a magazine tube extension and uses just a magazine cap as in the Model 870 shotgun. One has a round hole in the center; the other has a slot in the center. Put a screwdriver into the open end of the magazine tube. Move the tip under the rim of the magazine spring retainer. Place your hand over the end of the magazine tube. Using the screwdriver, pry up and remove the magazine spring retainer (Figure 2-10).

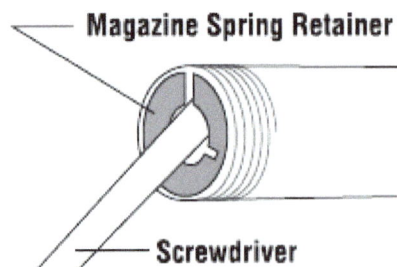

**Magazine Spring Retainer**

**Screwdriver**

**Figure 2-10**

C.  Remove the barrel.

**Figure 2-11a**                                      **Figure 2-11b**

Take hold of the barrel ahead of the magazine tube and pull the barrel from the receiver (Figures 2-11a and 2-11b).

D.  Remove the forearm.

**Figure 2-12 Press in the carrier.**

1.  Press in on the carrier (Figure 2-12).

 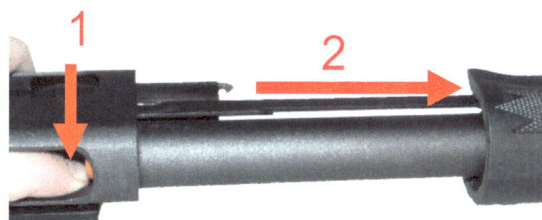

**Figure 2-13a**                                      **Figure 2-13b**

2.  Reach into the bottom of the receiver. Depress and hold the left shell latch (Figure 2-13a) while you slide the forearm forward and off of the magazine tube (Figure 2-13b).
    *   The top right edge of the slide may bind on the bottom front edge of the ejection port in the receiver. To free the slide, push the front end of the bolt down.

E. Remove the breech bolt assembly.

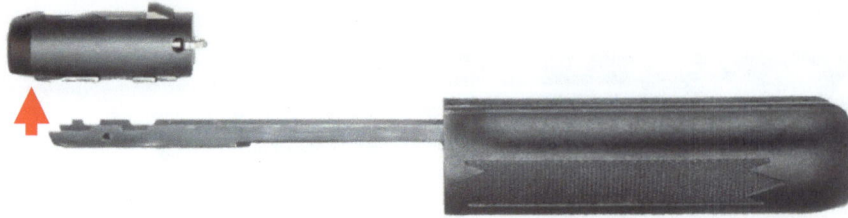

**Figure 2-14 Separate the breech bolt from the slide assembly.**

1. Lift the breech bolt assembly and slide assembly from the rear of the action bars (Figure 2-14).

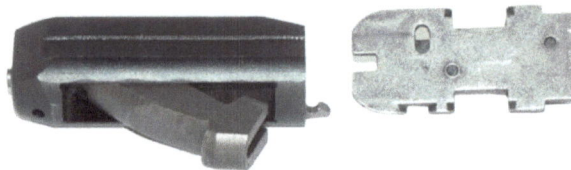

**Figure 2-15 Separate the bolt assembly.**

2. Separate the bolt assembly from the slide (Figure 2-15).

F. Remove trigger assembly from receiver.

**Figure 2-16a**            **Figure 2-16b**

1. Remove the front and rear trigger plate pins (Figures 2-16a and 2-16b). These photos show screws that attach the additional round carrier; stock shotguns have push pins.

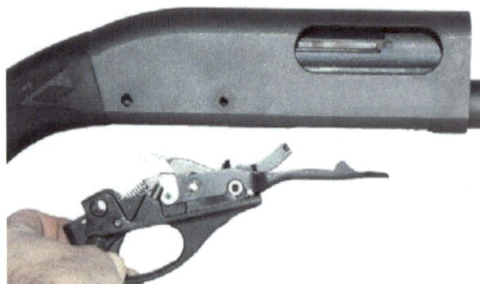

**Figure 2-17 Removing the trigger plate assembly.**

2. Lift the rear of the trigger plate assembly; slide rearward and remove from the receiver (Figure 2-17).

**WARNING! DO NOT** allow the hammer to snap forward when the trigger plate is removed. This can best be assured by keeping the safety mechanism engaged at all times. **RED BAND WILL NOT SHOW.**

## Cleaning and Lubrication

### To clean the barrel

1.  Select the correct gauge cleaning brush and attach the brush to the cleaning rod or select the correct sized BoreSnake.

2.  Put the brass cleaning brush into gun-cleaning solvent; dip the front (where the brass brushes are embedded) of the BoreSnake if this is used.

**Figure 2-18 Using a pull-through cleaning system.**

3.  Push the cleaning rod or pull the Boresnake through the barrel several times, from the chamber to muzzle (Figure 2-18).

4.  Push the correct size cleaning patch through the bore if using the cleaning rod method.

5.  Repeat several times using a clean patch each time until the patch is not dirty.

**Figure 2-19 Clean the locking notch.**

6.  Remove all shooting residue from the locking notch in the barrel (Figure 2-19).

## To clean the choke tubes, if present

1. Remove the choke tube from the barrel.

2. Clean the choke tube, including the threads, with gun-cleaning solvent and wipe dry. Apply light oil on threads and reassemble the choke tube to the barrel following the manufacturer's instructions.

## To clean the breech bolt assembly and slide assembly

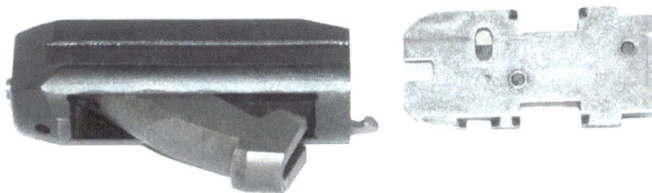

**Figure 2-20 Clean the bolt and slide assembly.**

Clean as a unit. Brush with cleaning solvent and wipe clean and dry (Figure 2-20).

## To clean the receiver

**Figure 2-21 Brush out the unburned powder in the receiver.**

Brush the inside of the receiver with cleaning solvent and wipe dry (Figure 2-21).

**WARNING-** There may be sharp edges inside the receiver. Keep fingers covered or gloved when wiping.

## To clean the trigger plate assembly

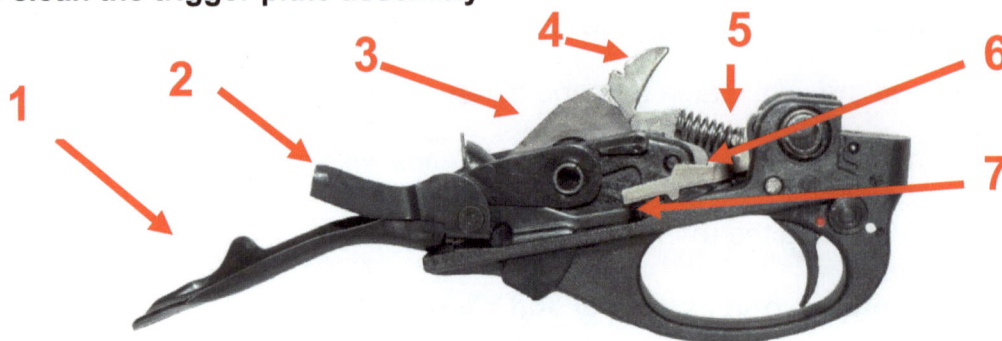

**Figure 2-22 Trigger plate assembly**

1- Carrier
2- Action Bar Lock
3- Hammer (Cocked)

4- Carrier Dog
5- Hammer Spring

6- Left Connnector
7- Disconnector

Clean as a unit with solvent. Let stand for 15 minutes so solvent can break down the fouling. Wipe with clean rags and wash off components with fresh solvent. Use compressed air and/or dry rags to remove the solvent. Lightly lubricate metal parts that make contact and must move against each other (Figure 2-22).

**NOTE**- Excessive use of a lubricant could adversely affect the function and safe operation of your firearm.

## Reassembling the Remington Shotgun

1. Check to make sure that the disconnector is below the end of the left connector.

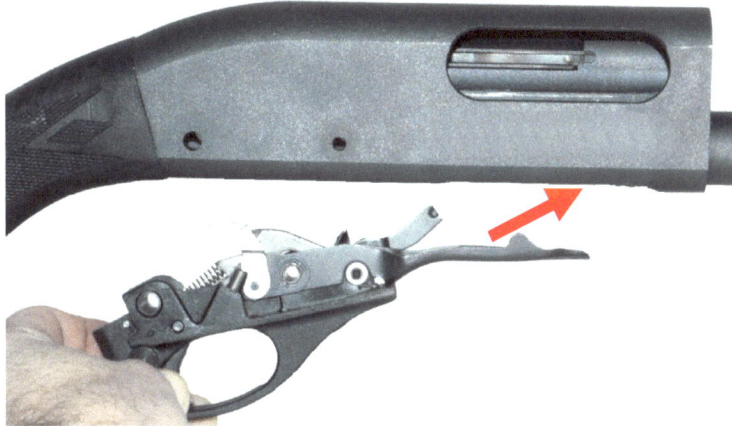

**Figure 2-23 Insert the trigger plate assembly.**

2. Carefully insert the trigger plate assembly (carrier first) into the receiver (Figure 2-23).

**Figure 2-24 Reinsert receiver pins/shell carrier bolt.**

3. Position to align the holes so you can insert the screws or tap in the front and rear trigger plate pins (Figure 2-24). Tighten up screws to the ammunition carrier; do not overtighten as it will deform the receiver and cause the action to fail.

**Figure 2-25 Position the fore-end assembly.**

4. Place the fore-end assembly over the magazine tube (Figure 2-25).

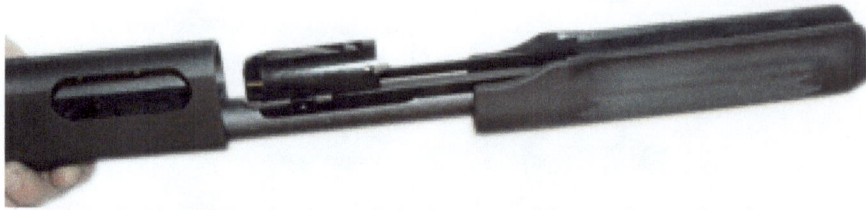

**Figure 2-26a Place the breech bolt assembly on the action bar assembly**

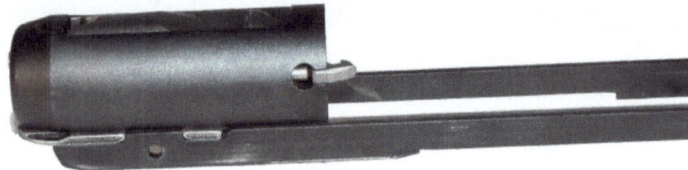

**Figure 2-26b Proper placement of the breech bolt assembly.**

5.  Place the breech bolt assembly on the block at the end of the action bar assembly (Figures 2-26a and 2-26b).

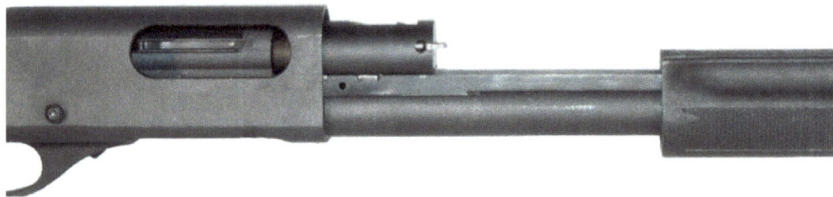

**Figure 2-27 Retract the forearm.**

6.  Guide the action bars into the receiver until stopped by the right shell latch (Figure 2-27).

**Figure 2-28 Depress the shell latches.**

7.  Push the carrier upward; depress and hold the right shell latch (Figure 2-28).

8.  Slide the fore-end rearward until stopped by the left shell latch.

**Figure 2-29**

9. Reach into the bottom of the receiver. Depress and hold the left shell latch (Figure 2-29).

10. Slide the forearm rearward until stopped by the action bar lock.

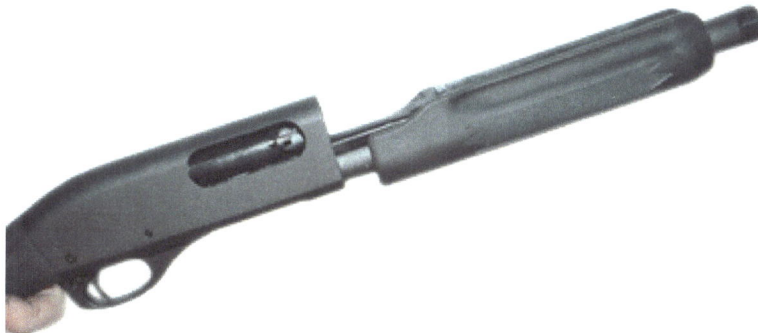
**Figure 2-30 Continue to the rear.**

11. Push upward on the action bar lock. Slide the forearm rearward approximately halfway (Figure 2-30).

**Figure 2-31a Place the barrel into the receiver.**

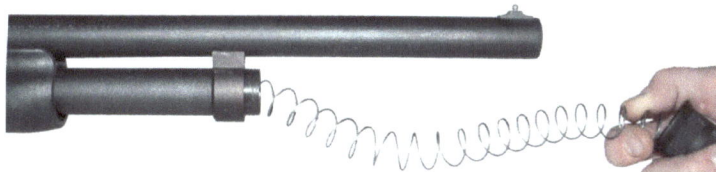
**Figure 2-31b Insert the spring into the magazine.**

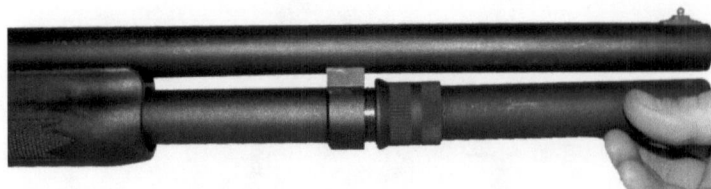

**Figure 2-31c Replace the barrel cap or magazine extension.**

12. Replace the barrel (Figure 2-31a), magazine spring (Figure 2-31b), and magazine cap/magazine tube extension (Figure 2-31c).

## Performing a Function Check on the Remington Shotgun

A.  Ensure the shotgun is clear of all ammunition and pointed in a safe direction.

B.  Position the forearm in the forward and locked position. Place the safety to the "**SAFE**" position (button pushed to the right and RED BAND NOT VISIBLE).

C.  Press the trigger (the hammer should not fall).

D.  Position the safety to the left (button will show the RED BAND) ("**FIRE**" position).

E.  Press the trigger (the hammer should fall).

F.  Release the trigger, actuate the forearm and return the forearm to the forward and locked position.

G.  Place the safety to the "**SAFE**" position (button pushed to the right and RED BAND NOT VISIBLE).

# Section 3

## Operation and Function

### Conditions of Carry

- **Condition One**- Action closed, chamber loaded, magazine tube loaded, weapon on **FIRE.**

- **Condition Two**- Action closed, chamber loaded, magazine tube loaded, weapon on **SAFE.**

- **Condition Three**- Action closed, chamber empty, magazine tube empty, weapon on **SAFE.**

- **Condition Four**- Action open (slide/bolt to the rear), chamber empty, magazine tube empty, weapon on **SAFE.**

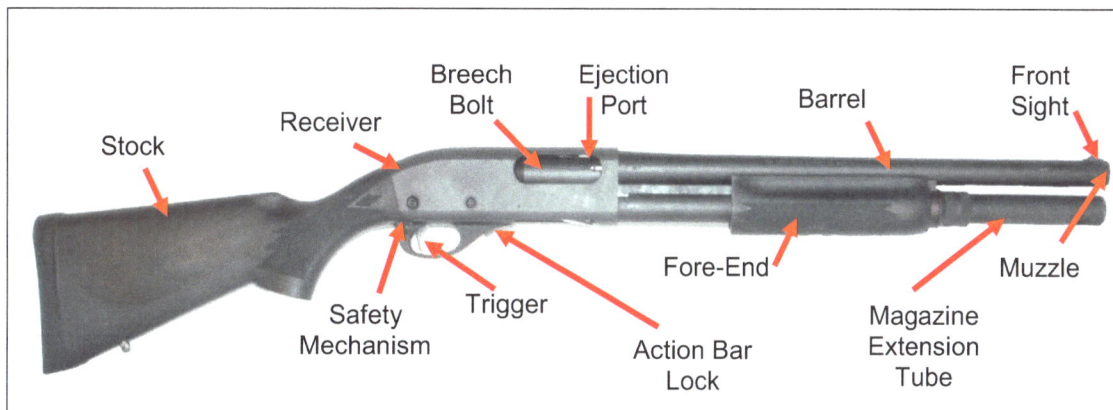

**Figure 3-1 Remington 870 nomenclature**

## Loading the Remington Shotgun

### To load the chamber and magazine (Condition One)

**Figure 3-2 Safe direction**

1. Point the shotgun in a safe direction (Figure 3-2).

2. Engage the safety mechanism. **RED BAND WILL NOT SHOW.**

3. Push upward on the action bar lock.

4. Pull the forearm fully rearward to open the action.

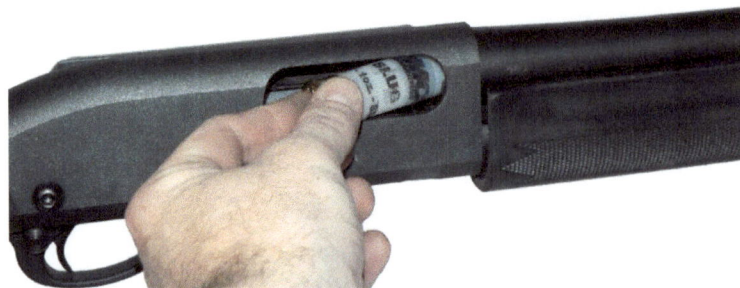

**Figure 3-3 Loading the chamber**

5.  Put one shell of the correct gauge and length through the ejection port into the chamber (Figure 3-3).

6.  Push the forearm forward to close and lock the action.

**NOTE- THE FIREARM IS NOW LOADED.**

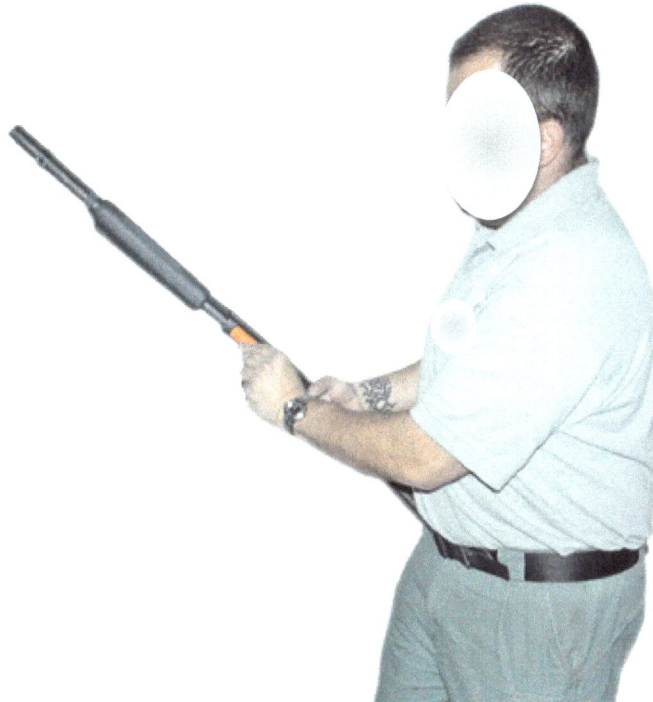

**Figure 3-4 Filling the magazine tube with shells**

7.  Press shells against the carrier and press them fully up into the magazine tube (Figure 3-4).

8.  Push the number of rounds desired or to capacity of the magazine tube on the shotgun, 3" or 2-3/4" shells of the correct gauge and length, one at a time, fully forward into the magazine.

**WARNING- BEFORE LOADING, ALWAYS CHECK THE BARREL MARKING FOR THE CORRECT GAUGE AND CHAMBER LENGTH. NEVER USE AMMUNITION WHICH EXCEEDS THE CHAMBER LENGTH SHOWN ON THE BARREL.**

**WARNING-** Be sure the rim of each shell snaps past the shell latch to prevent the shell from sliding back over the carrier.

If the shell slides back over the carrier,
• Engage the safety mechanism. Make sure the **RED BAND IS NOT SHOWING**.
• Keep the firearm pointed in a safe direction.
• Forcefully **OPEN** the action or

• **REMOVE** the trigger plate assembly following the disassembly instructions previously covered and remove the shell.

**To load only the magazine (Condition Two)**

1. Point the shotgun in a safe direction.

2. Engage the safety mechanism. **RED BAND WILL NOT SHOW.**

3. Push upward on the action bar lock.

4. Pull the forearm fully rearward to open the action.

5. Ensure the chamber and magazine tube has no ammunition.

6. Push the forearm forward to close and lock the action.

**NOTE- THE CHAMBER IS NOT LOADED.**

**Figure 3-5 Loading the magazine tube with shells**

7. Press shell against the carrier (Figure 3-5).

8. Push the number of rounds desired or to capacity of the magazine tube on the shotgun, 3" or 2-3/4" shells of the correct gauge and length, one at a time, fully forward into the magazine.

**WARNING- BEFORE LOADING, ALWAYS CHECK THE BARREL MARKING FOR THE CORRECT GAUGE AND CHAMBER LENGTH. NEVER USE AMMUNITION WHICH EXCEEDS THE CHAMBER LENGTH SHOWN ON THE BARREL.**

**WARNING-** Be sure the rim of each shell snaps past the shell latch to prevent the shell from sliding back over the carrier.

If the shell slides back over the carrier,
• Engage the safety mechanism. Make sure the **RED BAND IS NOT SHOWING**.
• Keep the firearm pointed in a safe direction.
• Forcefully **OPEN** the action or
• **REMOVE** the trigger plate assembly following the disassembly instructions previously covered and remove the shell.

## Firing the Remington Shotgun

**Figure 3-6 Oriented towards the threat area**

A. Orient downrange or towards the threat (Figure 3-6).

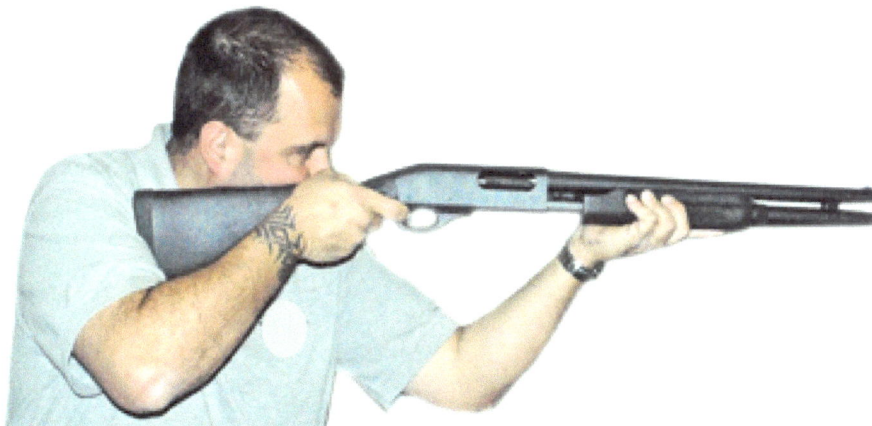

**Figure 3-7 Properly shouldered ready position with finger on safety button**

B. Push left on the safety button to release the safety with firing hand index finger (Figure 3-7).

**Figure 3-8 Properly shouldered ready position**

C. As you orient your sights onto the target, press the trigger straight back so as not to interrupt the sight picture (Figure 3-8) until the weapon fires. Do not pull the forearm to the rear with any force while firing as this will lock up the action, and you will have to push forward to unlock so you may chamber another round.

**Figure 3-9 Cycle the action after each shot**

D. Once the shot has been fired, release the trigger and actuate the forearm to the rear and back forward. To re-engage the threat, press the trigger straight to the rear and continue until you receive the desired effect (Figure 3-9).

E. When you have completed firing the Shotgun, place the safety lever into the SAFE (to the right) position.

# Section 4

## Performance Problems

### Malfunction and Immediate Action Procedures

Malfunctions are usually preventable through good practices, but they may still occur out of the blue from time to time. Of course, you hope it is on the practice range, but you should treat each one as though you are in a life-or-death situation. Practicing proper and effective corrective actions will allow you to be more confident in your shotgun handling. In stressful situations, you can become much more stressed due to an unforeseen malfunction that is easy to correct. I have observed many shooters that perceive themselves to be experienced, but when they encounter a stovepipe, they nearly disassemble the Shotgun rather than sweep it out and continue.

Malfunction drills must fix the problem 100% of the time (excluding a weapon stoppage—broken weapon) the first time performed. You must look at the shotgun and identify the problem (obviously the shotgun is not functioning as you need, so you must transition to another weapon or rectify the situation); it is a non-function weapon at this point—fix it.

You should always practice taking a covered position to correct malfunctions with considerations on how you operate.

The following pages in this chapter describe and detail corrective actions for the various malfunctions that may be encountered.

Practice all malfunctions, once understood, in situations as though the shooter is injured and one handed. Seek out proper instruction for shooting while wounded drills.

**NOTE**: The <u>failure-to-go-into-battery malfunction</u>, when your forearm does not fully forward when cycling a round, is always rectified in the same manner. Ensure the firearm is on "**SAFE**".

To fix a failure-to-go-into-battery malfunction, you must ensure your finger is off the trigger and outside the triggerguard and then attempt to chamber another round. If you have to, depress the action bar lock to actuate the slide to make this happen.

**FAILURE TO FIRE:** This malfunction occurs when the operator has loaded a dud cartridge or failed to load the chamber. The universal fix all for this is the "<u>Rack</u> and <u>Bang</u>" technique.

**SYMPTOM -** You perform a full presentation to shoot and hear and feel the hammer strike, and the weapon does not fire.

**Figure 4-1 Rack**

1. **RACK** the forearm to the rear and return to the forward position. Observe if a cartridge is ejected from the ejection port; maintain muzzle to threat orientation (Figure 4-1).

**Figure 4-2 Bang**

2. **BANG** or prepare to fire the shot as you intended before the malfunction if your situation dictates that action (Figure 4-2).

**FAILURE TO EJECT:** This malfunction (commonly called a "stovepipe") is created usually by the forearm being retarded (not fully pulling the fore-arm to the rear) in its rearward movement to rechamber the next round or a broken ejector. This malfunction is easily corrected by sweeping the expended case from the port.

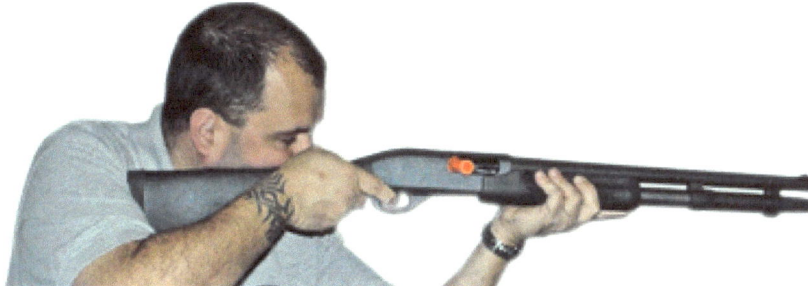
**Figure 4-3 Stovepipe**

**SYMPTOM -** You are in the act of shooting a multiple-round engagement and felt that the slide did not fully close and/or have a soft, mushy trigger (Figure 4-3).

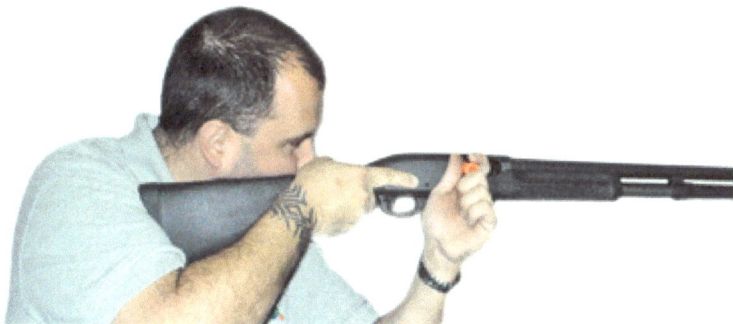
**Figure 4-4 Reach under**

Retract the forearm to the rear and with the non-firing hand, and reach under the receiver. Grasp the stuck/non-ejected casing to pull it free (Figure 4-4). Once the casing is removed from the ejection port, drop the casing.

**Figure 4-5 Completion of the sweep and cycling the next cartridge**

Once the casing is no longer pinched by the bolt, you will have to look to see if a loose round is on the carrier to be loaded into the chamber when the forearm is pushed forward. You are now ready to continue the engagement. If there is a cartridge in the magazine and not on the carrier, close the action, press the action bar lock and repump the action. The chamber will now be loaded. Many inexperienced shooters do too much to correct this simple malfunction. Continue the engagement as your situation dictates.

## Appendix A - **Ammunition**

The shotgun is a firearm typically used to fire a number of small spherical pellets called shot. These pellets cover a wider range than a rifle or pistol. The shot is usually fired from a smoothbore barrel; another configuration is the rifled slug barrel, which is used to fire a single projectile (though slugs can also be fired from smoothbore weapons). Since the power of the burning charge is divided among the pellets, the energy of any one ball of shot is fairly low, making shotguns useful primarily for hunting birds and other small game. However, the large number of projectiles makes the shotgun useful as a close-combat weapon or defensive weapon, where the short range ensures that many of the projectiles of shot will hit the target. Ammunition for shotguns is referred to as shotgun shells, shotshells, or shells. Single projectile loads are generally called shotgun slugs or slugs.

## Standard types include

• <u>Shot</u> (also known as birdshot in the smaller shot sizes) is the most commonly used round, filled with lead or lead substitute pellets. Shot shells are described by the size of the pellets within. Size Eight is the smallest size normally used for hunting and is used on small birds such as doves. Sizes Two, One, BB, BBB, and T are used for hunting large waterfowl such as geese. In Europe and in other "metric" countries, except Canada, the shot size is simply the diameter of the pellet given in millimeters.

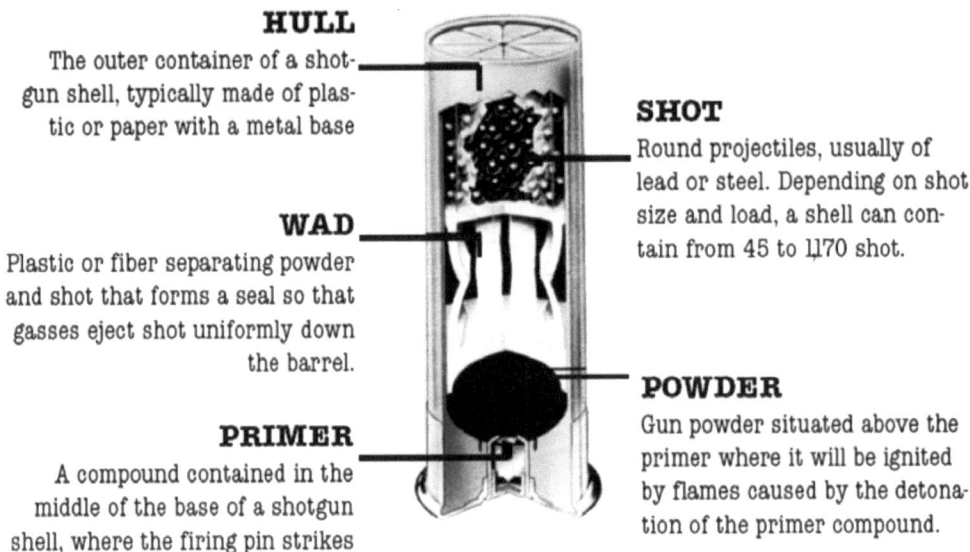

**HULL**
The outer container of a shotgun shell, typically made of plastic or paper with a metal base

**SHOT**
Round projectiles, usually of lead or steel. Depending on shot size and load, a shell can contain from 45 to 1,170 shot.

**WAD**
Plastic or fiber separating powder and shot that forms a seal so that gasses eject shot uniformly down the barrel.

**POWDER**
Gun powder situated above the primer where it will be ignited by flames caused by the detonation of the primer compound.

**PRIMER**
A compound contained in the middle of the base of a shotgun shell, where the firing pin strikes

**Figure A-1 Shotshell cutaway**

Table of Birdshot Size

| Size | Diameter | Pellets/oz Lead | Pellets/oz Steel |
|------|----------|-----------------|------------------|
| BBB | .190" (4.83 mm) | | 62 |
| BB | .180" (4.57 mm) | 50 | 72 |
| 1 | .160" (4.06 mm) | | 103 |
| 2 | .150" (3.81 mm) | 87 | 125 |
| 3 | .140" (3.56 mm) | | 158 |
| 4 | .130" (3.30 mm) | 135 | 192 |
| 5 | .120" (3.05 mm) | 170 | 243 |
| 6 | .110" (2.79 mm) | 225 | 315 |
| 7 1/2 | .100" (2.41 mm) | 350 | |
| 8 | .090" (2.29 mm) | 410 | |
| 9 | .080" (2.03 mm) | 585 | |

**Table A-1**

Buckshot is larger than birdshot and was originally designed for hunting larger game, such as deer. While the advent of new, more accurate slug technologies is making buckshot less attractive for hunting, it is still the most common choice for police, military, and home defense uses. Like birdshot, buckshot is described by pellet size, with larger numbers indicating smaller shot. From the smallest to the largest, buckshot sizes are: #4, (called "number four"), #1, 0, ("one-aught"), 00 ("double-aught"), 000 ("triple-aught"), and 0000 ("four-aught"). A common round for defensive use would be a 12-gauge 2¾" length 00 buck shell, which contains 8 balls of roughly .33 caliber. New "tactical" buckshot rounds, designed specifically for defensive use, use slightly fewer shot at lower velocity to reduce recoil and increase controllability of the shotgun.

## Table of Buckshot Size

| Size | Diameter | Pellets/oz |
|---|---|---|
| 000 or LG ("triple-aught") | .36" (9.1 mm) | 6 |
| 00 ("double-aught") | .33" (8.4 mm) | 8 |
| 0 or SG ("one-aught") | .32" (8.1 mm) | 9 |
| SSG | .31" (8.0 mm) | 12 |
| 1 | .30" (7.6 mm) | 10 |
| 2 | .27" (6.9 mm) | 15 |
| 3 | .25" (6.4 mm) | 18 |
| 4 | .24" (6.0 mm) | 21 |

**Table A-2**

• Slug rounds are rounds that fire a single solid slug. They are used for hunting large game and in certain military and law enforcement applications. Modern slugs are moderately accurate, especially when fired from special rifled slug barrels. They are often used in "shotgun-only" hunting zones near inhabited areas, where rifles are prohibited due to their excessive range.

## Specialty ammunition

The unique properties of the shotgun, such as large case capacity, large bore, and the lack of rifling, has led to the development of a large variety of specialty shells, ranging from novelties to high-tech military rounds.

• Bean bag rounds fire a nylon bag filled with birdshot or a similar loose, dense substance. The "punch" effect of the bag is useful for knocking down targets, and they are used by police to subdue violent suspects. The bean bag round is being phased out in favor of the "less lethal" rubber slug, as some bean bags catch the air much like a frisbee, which causes the denser seams of the bag to spin with enough force to slice through clothing, and often human flesh. These rounds are sometimes used by wildlife officials to non-lethally subdue wild animals. Bean bag rounds are also sold under the trademarked name of Flexible Baton Round.

- Bird bombs are low-powered rounds that fire a firecracker that is fused to explode a short time after firing. They are designed to scare animals, such as birds that congregate on airport runways.

- Blank shells contain only a small amount of powder and no actual load. When fired, the blanks provide the illusion of a real load, with most of the same characteristics, but no projectile leaves the gun barrel.

- Brenneke and Foster-type slugs have the same basic configuration as normal slugs, but have increased accuracy. The hollowed rear of the Foster slug improves accuracy by placing more mass in the front of the projectile, therefore inhibiting the "tumble" that normal slugs may generate. The Brenneke slug takes this concept a bit further with the addition of a wad that stays connected to the projectile after discharge, increasing accuracy. Both slugs are commonly encompassed by fins, which increase stability in flight.

- Disintegrator or Hatton rounds are designed to blow out deadbolts, door locks, and door hinges without risking the lives of those beyond the door. These rounds are packed with a mixture of dense metal powder (often lead) and wax, which can destroy a lock then immediately disperse. They are used by SWAT teams to force entry quickly into a locked room (Figure A-2).

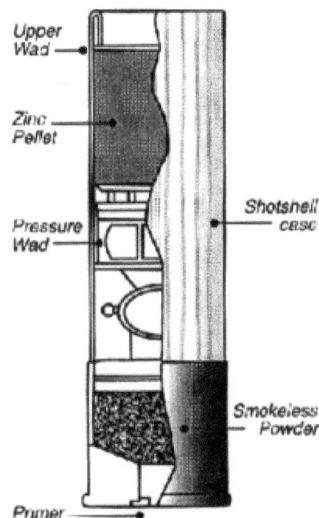

**Figure A-2 Breaching shell cutaway**

- <u>Flare</u> rounds are sometimes carried by hunters for safety and rescue purposes. They are available in low- and high-altitude versions. Some brands claim they can reach a height of up to 600 feet (180 m).

- <u>Flechette</u> rounds contain aerodynamic darts, typically from 8 to 20 in number. The flechette provides greatly extended range due to its aerodynamic shape and improved penetration of light armor. American troops during the Vietnam War packed their own flechette shotgun rounds, called *beehive rounds*, after the similar artillery rounds.

- <u>Gas</u> shells spray a cone of gas for several meters. These are primarily used by riot police. They normally contain pepper gas or tear gas. Other variations launch a gas grenade-like projectile.

- <u>Rubber fin stabilized projectiles, rubber slugs, and rubber buckshot</u> are similar in principle to the bean bag rounds. Composed of flexible rubber or plastic and fired at low velocities, these rounds are probably the most common choice for riot control. Shapes range from full-bore diameter cylinders to round balls of varying sizes (Figure A-3).

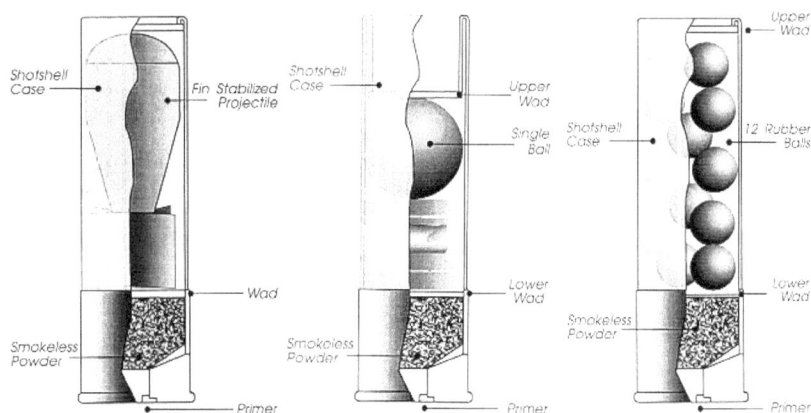

Figure A-3 Less lethal rubber projectiles

# Appendix B - Remington 870 Armorer Information

## Armorer's Checklist

1. Check function of shotgun with dummy shells (load, feed, lockup, extract, eject).
2. Check magazine cap (detent hole depth, oversized detent hole, threads).
3. Check barrel for damage (straightness, bulges, sights, chamber condition, magazine cap detent, barrel guide ring).
4. Check action tube, action bars, forearm assembly (bent, dents, cracked furniture, loose nut, binding or hard function).
5. Check bolt assembly (firing pin, firing pin retractor spring, extractor and extractor spring, locking bolt and retainer).
6. Check slide (solder joint, wear and condition).
7. Check stock and recoil pad (tightness, cracks and condition).
8. Check shell latches – right and left (spring tension).
9. Check magazine tube and receiver (dirt/fouling, dents, cracks, threads)
10. Check trigger plate assembly (dirt/fouling, rust, excessive oil, free & independent movement of left connector, bar lock & trigger, safety function, sear/hammer relationship).
11. Check shell latches – right and left (proper staking).
12. Check ejector and ejector spring (looseness, broken barrel locator, broken spring).
13. Check magazine spring, retainer, follower, and interior of magazine tube (kinks, looseness, cracked follower, new Orange follower installed).

Make notes of all faults or defects found during the disassembly. Repair or perform any needed maintenance prior to reassembly. If unable to repair, mark the firearm not for service and repair at first opportunity.

NOTE- Always perform the function testing with dummy shells, NEVER use live ammunition.

## Brownells Remington 870 Armorer's Tool Kit

1 - **870 FOREND WRENCH -** Pilot keeps "teeth" square to the forend nut, virtually eliminating damage to wrench, forend, or forend nut.

2 - **870 DETENT STAKING PUNCH -** Cutaway punch restakes the magazine cap retainer (detent ball) in place without forcing metal into the I.D. of the magazine ring.

3 - **870/1100 MAGAZINE SPRING RETAINER TOOL -** Guides springs into position without damage.

4 - **MENCK MAGAZINE CORKSCREW -** Threads into magazine spring retainer so you can "pop" it out like a cork.

5 - **870/1100 PIN PUSHER -** Fitted punch removes trigger group pins with no chance of slipping off and gouging the frame.

6 - **REMINGTON 870 RIVET STAKING TOOL SET -** Makes fitting the 870 ejector spring and housing onto Remington's 2-step rivet easy! Fastens the ejector housing to the lower portion of the rivet, then fits the upper part of the rivet to hold the ejector spring in the ejector housing.

7 & 18 - **870/1100 SHELL LATCH STAKER -** Our tool (7) has the correct, factory-designed, rectangular swaging point to displace plenty of metal and a built-in handle, plus lots of heft to take years of use. Includes Handi-Clamp (18) to hold ejector spring and housing secure when restaking.

8 - **870/1100 CARRIER PIVOT SLAVE PIN -** Greatly simplifies assembly of the trigger plate or "Fire Control Assembly." Tapered "nose" lines up Carrier, Carrier Dog Washer, and Trigger Plate. Carrier Pivot Tube fits onto "tail" of the Slave pin, follows it through and into place.

9 - **STARRETT PIN PUNCH -** Correct size for removing the Firing Pin Retaining Pin from the bolt assembly.

10 - **870 BUTTSTOCK BOLT WRENCH -** Special sleeved, self- centering bit can't slip off or jam between stock and bolt head. Mounted on 6" extension with T-Handle.

11 - **870/1100 SCREWDRIVER COMBO -** Our special Law Enforcement, MAGNA® Clip-Tip handle with 5 bits chosen for 870 work.

12 - **REMINGTON 870 OWNER'S MANUAL -** Factory, 22-page manual has full instructions on Safety, Parts Identification and Assembly, Loading/Unloading, Cleaning, plus an exploded view drawing and full parts list. Furnished with kit only. Not available separately from Brownells.

13 - **1" NYLON/BRASS HAMMER -** The Brass head and 6 oz. weight is perfect for driving the various punches supplied in the 870 Armorer's Kit. Nylon head provides a no-mar "tap."

14 - **ARMORER'S BRUSH -** Perfect shape and stiffness for removing metal filings, abrasive stone dust, etc., from recesses.

15 - **MF-46 MEDIUM INDIA STONE -** Removes burrs and roughness for smoother functioning.

16 - **ASSEMBLY/DISASSEMBLY MAT -** Solvent/oil-resistant, no-slip, no-scratch work surface. Rolls up for easy carrying.

17 - **GUN/PARTS CLEANING BRUSH -** Solvent-proof polypropylene brush for hard scrubbing. Narrow row for grooves and slots; toothbrush end for general scrubbing.

19 - **870 SERVICE KIT BOX -** Roomy, Field Tool Box with the distinctive 870 Service Kit label. Holds all the Kit tools easily, with room left over for personal favorites. Oil and solvent-proof.